We Laughed A Lot, My First Day Of School

by Sylvia Root Tester
illustrated by Frances Hook

THE CHILD'S WORLD

ELGIN, ILLINOIS 60120

Library of Congress Cataloging in Publication Data

Tester, Sylvia Root, 1939-
  We laughed a lot, my first day of school.

  SUMMARY: Scared to go to his first day of
kindergarten, Juan discovers it's not so bad—he
even laughs a lot.
  [1. Kindergarten—Fiction] I. Hook, Frances.
II. Title.
PZ7.T288WI   [E]   78-10900
ISBN 0-89565-020-7

Distributed by Childrens Press, 1224 West Van Buren Street, Chicago,
Illinois 60607.

We Laughed A Lot, My First Day Of School

I didn't want to go,
my first day of school.

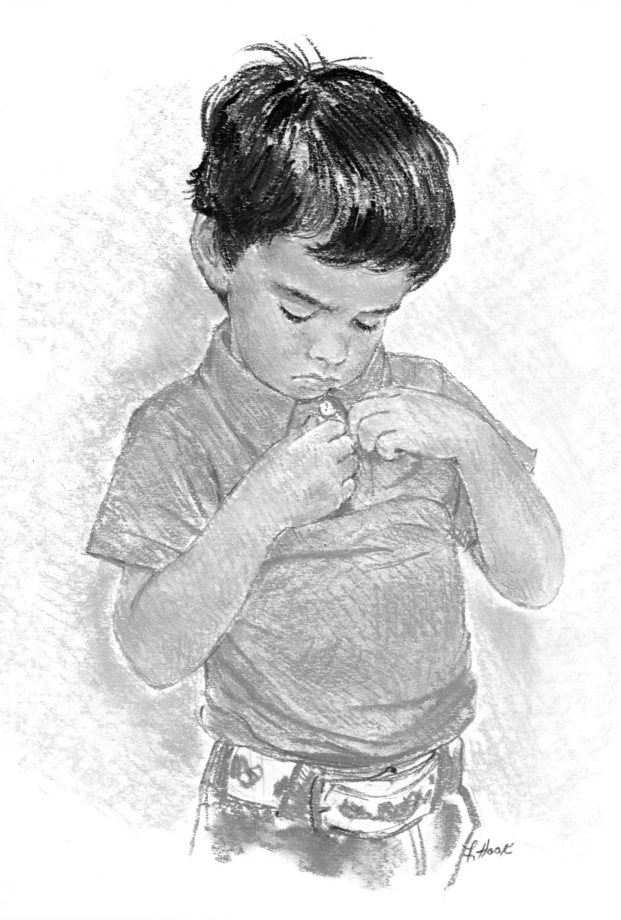

I thought of telling my father,
but he said,
"Ahh, my oldest son!
Your first day of school!
I am so proud.
In Mexico, I could not
go to school very much.
I had to work.
But here, in the United States,
for you, my son, it will be better."

10

I thought of telling my mother,
but she said,
"Look at you!
How handsome you are!
Oh, we are proud, so very proud.
You will do well,
your first day at school."

I thought of telling my friend Jamie,
but it was her first day too.
So I didn't tell anyone
how scared I was.

13

"Hello, Juan. Hello, Jamie," said the teacher.
He stooped down and looked right at us.
Then he smiled—big.
I had to smile too.
"Maybe the first day won't be too bad,"
I said to Jamie.

And it wasn't.
The teacher-man told me his name.
It was Mister Green.
He let me look in his pocket
for a surprise.

It was a crayon.
"A green crayon," he said.
"So you'll remember my name."
But I won't forget his name.
He is my first teacher.
And he likes me.

I colored with the crayon.
You know what?
It was grass color!
Green is grass color!

Then I played with the milk trucks.
Soon I had a whole row of trucks —
milk trucks and gas trucks
and dump trucks.
A great big truck parade!

We sang songs and danced dances.
Jamie was good at the dances.
And we laughed a lot.

We even went outside and played.
I liked the jungle gym best.
I hung upside down.
The other children looked as if they were standing on their heads.

Later, Mr. Green read a book to us.
It was funny.
Mr. Green made faces like the clown.
Then we did too.

Before I knew it,
my first day of school was over.
"I was scared," said Jamie,
"but it was OK."
"I wasn't," I said.
"I'm not scared of anything!"
"Yeah, sure," said Jamie,
and she laughed.
So I laughed too.
We laughed all the way home,
after our first day of school.

About the Artist

Frances Hook was educated at the Pennsylvania Museum School of Art in Philadelphia, Pennsylvania. She and her husband, Richard Hook, worked together as a free-lance art team for many years, until his death. Within the past 15 years, Mrs. Hook has moved more and more into the field of book illustrating.

Mrs. Hook has a unique ability for capturing the moods and emotions of children. She has this to say about her work. "Over the years, I have centered my attention on children. I've done many portraits of children. I use children in the neighborhood for my models. I never use professional models."

A great admirer of Mary Cassatt, an American Impressionist, Mrs. Hook enjoys doing fine art as well as commercial work.

About the Author

Sylvia Root Tester has been writing for children for twenty years. She has written fairy tales, folk tales, fantasy, science fiction and real-life stories, as well as supplemental teaching books. In addition, she has written works for teachers and for parents. As her own children were growing up, she tried out her stories on them. Now she uses nephews and nieces as her sounding board.

"I enjoy writing for children," she says. "If I can spark a child's imagination, or if I can make a child say, 'Yes, that's the way it is,' I've done my job."

E   Day school   019753
Tes
Tester
We laughed a lot, my first day
of school